Get Wise

Relationships

➔ how can we get them right?

Jane Bingham and Sarah Medina

Heinemann
LIBRARY

www.heinemann.co.uk/library

Visit our website to find out more information about **Heinemann Library** books.

To order:

☎ Phone 44 (0) 1865 888066

🖹 Send a fax to 44 (0) 1865 314091

💻 Visit the Heinemann Bookshop at www.heinemann.co.uk/library to browse our catalogue and order online.

First published in Great Britain by Heinemann Library, Halley Court, Jordan Hill, Oxford OX2 8EJ, part of Harcourt Education.

Heinemann is a registered trademark of Harcourt Education Ltd.

Editorial: Lucy Thunder and Harriet Milles
Design: David Poole and Kamae Design
Illustrations: Jeff Anderson
Picture Research: Melissa Allison and Kay Altwegg
Production: Camilla Smith

Originated by Ambassador Litho Ltd
Printed and bound in China, by WKT Company Limited

The paper used to print this book comes from sustainable resources.

ISBN 0 431 21036 5
09 08 07 06 05
10 9 8 7 6 5 4 3 2 1

British Library Cataloguing in Publication Data

Bingham, Jane; Medina, Sarah
(Get Wise). – Relationships – how can we get them right?
302

A full catalogue record for this book is available from the British Library.

Acknowledgements

The Publishers would like to thank the following for permission to reproduce photographs:
pp. **4**, **15** Getty Images/Photodisc; pp. **5**, **16**, **24** Education Photos; p. **6** Powerstock/Zave Smith; pp. **7**, **9**, **12** Corbis/Royalty Free; p. **8** Bubbles/Ian West; p. **10** Bubbles/Geoff du Feu; pp. **13**, **20**, **23** Alamy/Royalty Free p. **14** www.JohnBirdsall.co.uk; p. **17** Bubbles/Chris Rout; p. **22** Bubbles/Angela Hampton; p. **25** Alamy/Steve Skjold; p. **27** Alamy/ Wolffy

Talk time images pp. **5**, **11**, **13**, **21**, **25**, **29** Getty Images/Photodisc

Cover photograph reproduced with permission of Alamy/Image 100

The Publishers would like to thank Dr Ute Navidi, former Head of Policy at ChildLine, for her assistance in the preparation of this book.

Every effort has been made to contact copyright holders of any material reproduced in this book. Any omissions will be rectified in subsequent printings if notice is given to the Publishers.

Disclaimer

Contents

Words appearing in bold, **like this**, are explained in the Glossary.

What are relationships all about?

A relationship is a kind of connection. Every day, you connect with a range of people – with your family, your friends and your teachers, but also with **acquaintances**, such as shopkeepers. In fact, each time you talk to someone, you form some kind of relationship with them. Can you think how many people you talked to today?

Relationships matter

Relationships are at the centre of everyone's life. They can bring great happiness – and sometimes sadness, too. Good relationships make you feel special and loved. They also help you to feel good about yourself and others. Happy relationships can even keep you healthy!

Friendship makes life fun, and having different friends makes life interesting, too!

Talk time

Who do you have relationships with?

Rick: Scott's my best friend – I feel I can trust him with all my secrets.

Tanvi: I'm really close to my older sister. She seems to understand just how I feel.

Lei-Lei: I like my teacher and I **respect** him too.

Scott: My grandad's loads of fun to be with, and he always has time for me.

Fact Flash

Scientific surveys show that people with healthy relationships live longer and are less likely to suffer from serious illnesses such as **cancer** and heart disease.

It's not always easy

Sometimes, relationships can be difficult. People are not always easy to get along with. Even with your closest friends, there can be times when you rub each other up the wrong way. A good, strong relationship needs plenty of give and take.

This book takes a good look at different kinds of relationships and how they work. It also gives you lots of ideas on how to keep your relationships strong and happy.

🎧 Some of our relationships are very close, but some are with people we don't know so well.

Making relationships work

What are the secrets of a good relationship?

People have lots of different kinds of relationships. Some are very close, such as the relationships with family and friends. Others are more distant. However, all relationships need some special effort to make them work well.

I like you just the way you are

One of the most important things in any relationship is to accept that everyone is different. Don't always expect other people to be just like you! Try to enjoy their differences and **respect** them for being who they are. After all, if everyone was exactly the same, it would make life pretty boring!

It's good to talk

Getting along with other people is mostly about **communicating**. That means talking and listening too. Your family and friends will like to share their news and feelings with you. They will also want to hear what is happening to you.

🔊 You can get along with all sorts of people if you remember to concentrate on their good points.

Trust in me

All good relationships are based on trust. Your friends need to know that they can trust you to keep a secret, that you will support them – and that you won't be mean about them behind their backs.

Sometimes, a friend might want to talk to you about their problems. If your friends have something that is worrying them, it is important for them to know that they can trust in you.

Sophie's story

Sophie has been best friends with Nabila for the past three years. This is her story.

'When I first met Nabila I didn't think we'd be friends. We were just so different! But then we got talking and I realized she was really good fun. Now we do loads of things together. I feel I can really talk to her and we're always texting each other! Sometimes we quarrel about little things, but we soon make up, and we try to support each other if one of us is unhappy.'

🎧 You can have relationships with people of all ages – and each one is different and special.

THINK IT THROUGH

Can relationships ever be perfect?

Yes. Sometimes two people really 'click' and they never fall out.

No. Even the best of friendships need to be worked at.

What do YOU think?

Can the way you feel about yourself affect your relationships with other people?

If you want your relationships to work really well, one of the first things you need to do is to make sure you have a good relationship with yourself! This means feeling happy with the person you are, and not wanting to change yourself. It is called having good **self-esteem**. A good self-esteem will make you happier, more confident and much more fun to be with.

I'm OK, you're OK

It's very important to respect and **value** other people – but you should feel good about yourself, too. Everyone has their good points and their not-so-good points! If you get to know yourself and accept the way you are, then it will be easier for you to accept other people. You will realize that nobody is perfect – and that's OK!

TOP TIPS

Having good self-esteem means that you:

◎ value yourself
◎ know what you like
◎ recognize your good and bad points
◎ are kind to yourself
◎ forgive yourself if you make a mistake.

And having good self-esteem helps you to build strong, healthy relationships with others!

If you know the things that you enjoy, it will help you find friends with similar interests.

Be true to yourself

Sometimes it is tempting to change the way you behave, just to make other people like you more. But, in the end, this won't make anyone happy. It is impossible to have a real friendship with someone who is pretending to be something they are not! It is much better to let your friends know the 'real you'. Then they can like you for who you really are.

◔ Feeling good about yourself is catching – it makes everyone feel better!

THINK IT THROUGH

Is it selfish or vain to like yourself?

Yes. You should think about others, not yourself.

No. Having good self-esteem helps you get on better with other people.

What do YOU think?

What makes a family – and what kind of relationships do you have with your family?

F or most young people, their closest relationships are with their family – their parents or **carers**, and their brothers and sisters. Grandparents and **step-parents** can also be very close. But what exactly is a family?

Families today

Families today take many different forms. Some children live with just one parent. Others share their time between their mum and their dad, and many children live in **step-families.** Some children and young people are looked after by carers that are not their parents, such as grandparents. And some children live in **extended families**, where parents and childre live together with other relatives.

Family feelings

Families can give you great love, friendship and support – bu family life can also be quite challenging, with lots of ups and downs. It can be easy to get annoyed with people in your family, because you have to get on with them every day.

Fact Flash

In the UK and Australia, approximately 1 in 5 families with children are step-families.

More and ➲ more children nowadays live with just one parent – and this small family is just as important as any other.

Sometimes, it ca take a lot of effo to get along wel with the people who are closest to you. Howeve it is perfectly normal to have some argumen in families.

Talk time

Are our family relationships the most important?

Rick: My dad's always nagging me to tidy my room.

Tanvi: Same here! And he won't let me stay out late with my friends.

Lei-Lei: My younger sister's really annoying sometimes. She wants to do everything I do.

Scott: When my uncle comes to visit, he always makes fun of my clothes and hair.

Matthew's story

Matthew lives with his brothers and sisters, his parents and his grandmother. His uncle and aunt and cousins live just down the road.

'When Mum and Dad are busy at work, my Gran looks after me, or sometimes I go to my auntie's house. I like having a big family because there's always someone to do things with. If I have a row with Mum and Dad, Gran talks to me and makes me feel much better.'

TOP TIPS

Sometimes family relationships can go seriously wrong and even become violent. If that happens, it is very important to ask for help. There are 24-hour helplines that children can ring if they feel **threatened** or **bullied** at home. You can find details of these on page 31 of this book.

THINK IT THROUGH

Are our family relationships the most important?

Yes. Nobody knows you better than your family, and nobody loves you as much.

No. You could manage fine without your family.

What do YOU think?

How can you
get on well with
the adults in
your life?

Some of the most important relationships you will
have are with your parents or **carers**. You may
also have a special relationship with another adult in
your family, such as a grandparent. Your relationships
with these adults will be very different from your
friendships with people your own age.

TOP TIPS

Remember that your
parents or carers want
what is best for you. If
you don't agree with
what they say, try
talking to them calmly
about what you think
or want, and why.

Parents and carers

Parents and carers can teach their children lots of important
things about life, and about getting on with other people.
They can show great love and acceptance, even when not
everyone in the family is behaving well! However, it is hard
to get on well all the time, and it can be easy for parents
and children to get angry and impatient with each other.

Because parents and carers
love their children, they
worry about them a lot.
Sometimes they may seem
bossy, or just too curious
about what is going on.
But really parents simply
want to know that their
children are safe
and happy.

◔ With your family, you
can be yourself – and
this can make it one of
your most comfortable
relationships.

It's good to talk

As children get older, they may start to question their parents more. There may be more arguments at home. This is perfectly normal. Good **communication** – listening as well as talking – will help to sort out most problems between parents and children.

Talk time

How do you get on with your parents or carers?

Rick: I love my dad, but I wish he didn't always want to know what I'm doing.

Tanvi: I know what you mean. Sometimes my mum really stresses out at me.

Lei-Lei: My auntie's just the same. But at other times, she's really fun to be with.

Scott: My gran is great, but I wish she wouldn't fuss about me all the time.

🎧 Sometimes it can help to turn to a grandparent or an aunt or uncle for support and understanding.

THINK IT THROUGH

Are relationships with parents or carers easy?

Yes. They are your closest relatives, so of course you will get on with them!

No. It needs lots of give and take to make family relationships work.

What do YOU think?

How can relationships with brothers and sisters work well?

Do you have brothers or sisters, or **step-brothers** or **step-sisters**, at home? And are they your friends? Relationships with **siblings** are often close – but that doesn't mean they are always easy.

Oh brother!

Siblings can be ready-made friends – really good mates who always look out for one another. Unfortunately, it does not always work out like this. Sometimes, brothers and sisters may be jealous of each other. They may deliberately tease and annoy each other. Or they may just be thoughtless and take each other for granted.

❶ Relationships are often about give and take. This can mean sharing things with a brother or sister or a step-sibling.

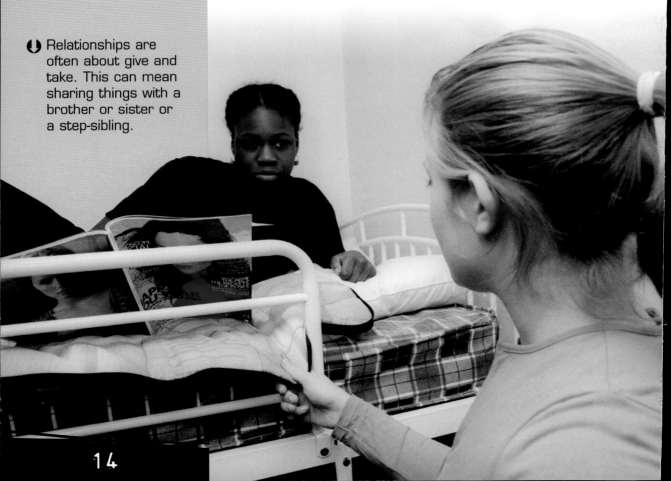

🎧 Taking time to talk things over with your siblings – or even help them out – can bring you closer.

We're all in this together

Although you can't choose your siblings like you do your friends, you can learn ways to get along with them. Next time you feel annoyed with your brother or sister, make a deliberate effort not to get into a fight. Take a deep breath and try talking calmly instead.

If you talk together about the things you each find difficult, you might be able to find some ways to make your lives easier. Sometimes, just seeing your brother or sister's point of view can help you to change your behaviour – and that has to be better than arguing all the time!

Time out

Some problems between siblings are caused by spending too much time together. Try to respect each other's privacy and spend some time apart.

Will you be my friend?

How do people choose their friends – and what makes a good friendship?

Fact Flash

During their lifetime, people may have around 350 mates – but only six of these are true friends.

Family relationships are very important, but we all need friends, too. We can't choose our families – but we can choose our close friends, so it is very important to make good choices!

Different friends

Friends can simply be people who we see often. But we have closer friends, too, and these are people we like very much. Our closest, best friends can be very special to us. Some close friendships can last a lifetime.

Sharing things

What makes two people become close friends? Often, friends share the same interests. There is always lots to talk about when friends play the same sport or like the same programmes on TV. However, not all friends like exactly the same things – they can also enjoy learning new things from each other.

Joining clubs or ➲ doing activities you enjoy is a great way to meet new people and make new friends!

We just click

One of the main reasons why people chose their friends is because of their **personalities**. Some of your friends may be lively and funny, and some may be quieter and good to talk to. Not all your friends have to be the same – and they don't have to have the same personality as you. What matters most is feeling really comfortable with each other, and knowing you can always trust your friend.

TOP TIPS

It can be hard to take the first steps towards a new friendship, but it is definitely worth it. Here are some suggestions:

◎ Don't be afraid to talk to new people. You will probably find they are really pleased that you made the first step.

◎ Try talking about the things you like to do. The chances are you will find someone else who likes them too.

◎ When you meet new people, don't forget to ask them about the things they like. Most people really enjoy talking about their interests.

◎ Once you have got to know someone a little, you could suggest doing something together – it is a great way to help your friendship grow.

⋒ Good friends are there for each other in the good times as well as the bad.

THINK IT THROUGH

Can you have lots of best friends?

Yes. You can easily spread yourself around lots of different mates.

No. It takes time to get to know a friend really well.

What do YOU think?

Are you a good friend?

Do you think you are a good friend – even the very best of friends? Try this fun quiz to check out how good a friend you really are. All the questions can work for boys and girls. Answers and helpful hints are printed upside down on the opposite page.

1 *Your friend arrives at school looking very upset. Do you...*
  a Carry on as usual, and hope she will feel better soon.
  b Tell her to cheer up and look on the bright side.
  c Ask her gently if she would like to talk to you about anything.

2 *You and your friend have made special plans for Saturday. You know he is looking forward to it, but then you get an invitation to another mate's party. Do you...*
  a Say yes to the party and tell your friend you will see him some other time.
  b Stick to your original plans with your friend.
  c Accept the invitation and tell your friend you have to do something important with your family.

3 One of your friends doesn't wear fashionable clothes, and your other mates make fun of her. Do you...

a Stick up for your friend. It is **personality** that counts, not clothes.

b Walk away from your other mates when they start to make fun.

c Join in with your other mates. After all – your friend is not there to hear you.

4 One day, your friend says he just wants to be alone. Do you...

a Tell him to snap out of it.

b Ask him why he wants to be on his own.

c Respect his privacy and give him some space, but ask him if he would like to see you later.

Answers and suggestions:

Q1 The best choice is (c), but you need to go very gently. Sometimes people don't feel able to talk about what is upsetting them. Just be patient, and your friend may decide to talk to you later.

Q2 A good friend would chose (b). In the long run, the most important thing is your friendship, not the party. And it never pays to tell lies, as in option (c). If your friend found out you had lied to him, he would be even more upset!

Q3 If you are a loyal friend, the answer must be (a). But if your friend wants to look more fashionable, you could always lend her some of your clothes.

Q4 You should go for (c). It is tempting to ask your friend why he wants to be alone, but he can always tell you later if he wants to.

How do arguments start – and how do friends make up again?

Do you ever fall out with your friends? Most people do, at one time or another. One of your friends might feel jealous or angry with you. Or they might simply misunderstand something you said. However an argument starts, it can leave you both feeling very upset.

Making up

Nobody wants to quarrel, but often arguments can give you the chance to talk about things that matter to you. Even though it can be hurtful to argue with a friend, it is possible to make it up again. Once you have had a chance to think things over, you will probably see that there are faults on both sides. If you are prepared to say you are sorry and talk things over calmly together, you should be able to become good friends again.

Sometimes ➲ falling out and making up again can make a friendship stronger.

It's all over

Sometimes friendships come to a natural end. Perhaps one person moves away or goes to a different school. This makes it harder to stay in touch. Friends can just grow apart, too. You might each develop separate interests, or you might decide that you want to spend your time with different people.

Talk time

What kind of things do friends fall out over?

Scott: I was angry with my mate when he told me I was rubbish at football.

Rick: Yeah, I remember that. And I got mad with my friend for leaving me out of his team.

Tanvi: My mate didn't keep her promise to help me with my homework.

Lei-Lei: And my friend never rang me when I was ill, even though I was away from school all week.

THINK IT THROUGH

Should you have to make an effort to keep your friends?

Yes. It is definitely worth trying to get over any arguments and misunderstandings.

No. Once you have fallen out with someone, the friendship is over.

What do YOU think?

Luke's story

Luke and Leo were best friends in primary school. Then Leo's family moved away.

'I missed Leo a lot, but we kept on phoning and texting each other, and sometimes we sent each other jokes by e-mail. In the holidays, I went to stay with him. He showed me around his town and I met his new friends. It was great to know we could still have fun together.'

How do relationships between girlfriends and boyfriends work?

As children get older, they may want to have a special friend – a girlfriend or boyfriend just for them. This is a natural part of growing up. Having a girlfriend or boyfriend can make young people feel very special, and it can be good fun too.

There's no rush

Sometimes, young people can feel left out because they don't have a girlfriend or boyfriend. But there is no need to rush. There is plenty of time to find a special friend.

Keeping a balance

If you do have a girlfriend or boyfriend, it is very important to keep time for your family and other friends, too. Just because there is someone new in your life, it is a real shame to stop having fun with your family and mates.

It is fun to have a ➲ lot of friends, both girls and boys.

Splitting up

Some relationships between girlfriends and boyfriends don't last very long. After a while together, you may find out that you do not really have that much in common. Splitting up can be much easier if you have kept in touch with your other friends.

Anna's story

Anna spent so much time with her boyfriend that she hardly saw her other friends. Then things went wrong …

'Ben and I were crazy about each other. We did everything together, and when we had to be apart we were always texting each other! I didn't have time for any of my other friends, and after a while they stopped asking me to do things with them.

'Then Ben and I split up. I was really lonely – and I'd lost touch with all my friends. Gradually, I got back together with my mates and started going out with them again. But it took a while … I'm never going to let that happen again.'

It can be great to have a special friend, but it is important not to lose touch with your other friends.

THINK IT THROUGH

Does having a girlfriend or boyfriend make you 'cool'?

Yes. It is good for your image to have a 'special' friend.

No. Being cool is about your own **personality** – not about your boyfriend or girlfriend.

What do YOU think?

People all around us

How do we treat the people we meet everyday?

We all meet many people in our daily lives, and not all of them become our friends. But even if you see someone for just a short time, you still have a relationship with them.

People at school

At school, you have a relationship with your teachers. They expect you to be polite and to treat them with **respect**. This means not shouting out in class and waiting until your teacher has time to talk to you. It also means not asking **personal** questions about their life at home. Your relationship with your teacher is quite different from your relationship with your family and friends.

There are many other people at school who you need to get along with, even if they are not your friends. If you are thoughtful and **cooperative**, everything will run more smoothly, and your time at school will be more enjoyable.

TOP TIPS

Always think before you say or do something that could hurt someone else! Remember everyone has feelings, just like you.

The relationship ➲ between a pupil and teacher can be special.

Other people

During your daily life you will meet many **acquaintances** – people like neighbours or shopkeepers, who you stop to talk to for just a few minutes. It is important to respect everyone you meet, and to be polite to them – just as you would want them to show respect for you.

Talk time

What kinds of people do you meet in your everyday lives?

Tanvi: I often stop to say hello to the old lady at the end of my street.

Rick: Sometimes I have a chat with the man who runs our local shop.

Lei-Lei: On Sundays, I talk to the people who go to my church.

Scott: I see my football coach twice a week.

🎧 Even if you don't know someone really well, it is important to be polite to them. And it makes everyone feel better, too!

THINK IT THROUGH

Should people be able to treat others just as they want to?

Yes. You should feel free to talk to people however you like.

No. Everyone deserves to be treated with respect.

What do YOU think?

Why are talking and listening so important in relationships?

Top thoughts

'The secret to friendship is being a good listener.'

Old saying

Relationships with others – family, friends, boyfriends and girlfriends – can sometimes go wrong. One of the main reasons for this is a breakdown in **communication**. Communication means talking and listening – which sounds easy enough. But sometimes it can be surprisingly hard to get through to somebody else.

That's not what I meant!

It is not always easy to say exactly what you mean. You may find it hard to say what you want to, because you feel embarrassed or shy. Or you may imagine that someone else should know exactly what you think, without you having to say it out loud. Either way, not talking about your feelings can make you feel lonely and misunderstood.

You're just not listening!

Listening to other people is important, too. Even if someone is telling you clearly how they feel, it is not always easy to be a good listener. Sometimes you may be so busy talking yourself that you don't really hear what someone else is saying to you. Or you may decide that you already know what the other person wants, and so you don't bother to listen carefully.

In all relationships, it is very important for each person to feel they have been listened to. Listening to someone shows them that you **value** their feelings and opinions.

When you listen properly to other people it makes them feel that their opinions really matter. This can often make them feel better all round.

TOP TIPS

Follow these tips to become a better listener:

◎ Try to listen more than you talk.
◎ Don't interrupt the other person.
◎ Give the other person time to think.
◎ Think carefully about what is being said to you.
◎ Try to respond to what the other person actually says – not to what you expect them to say!

THINK IT THROUGH

Should you listen more than you talk?

Yes. That way you will get to know what the other person really thinks.

No. The most important thing is getting your own views across.

What do YOU think?

27

How can you make your relationships work really well?

Relationships are so important in our lives that we all need to do our best to get them right. Luckily, there are lots of things we can do to help our relationships work well.

Feeling good

An important key to healthy relationships with others is feeling good about yourself. If you have good **self-esteem** and accept the way you are, then you will get on much better with other people. It is also very important for your friends and family to know that you accept them and **value** them for what they are.

Two-way trust

When you feel that you can really trust someone else, you can relax and enjoy your relationship. In a trusting relationship, you know that you can both rely on each other. And the more you prove you are a trustworthy friend, the more your friends will feel close to you.

Top thoughts

'Love makes the world go round.'

Old saying and Madonna song.

The world would ➲ be a lonely place without friends and family to share life's ups and downs.

What would it be like to have no friends or family?

Tanvi: I'd be incredibly lonely without my family — they give me so much support.

Rick: Mine too — and I'd really miss talking things through with my friends.

Scott: Life wouldn't be any fun without my mates. Who would I have a laugh with?

Lei-Lei: And I'd even miss my annoying little sister!

Keep on communicating

Keeping relationships alive and healthy is all about **communicating**. Always try to let your friends know what you are feeling, and listen very carefully to what they say to you.

So long as you keep talking and listening to each other, you are a long way along the road to getting your relationships right!

THINK IT THROUGH

Do we really need other people?

Yes. We need other people to support us in the tough times and to share the good times, too.

No. Relationships are too much like hard work. We can manage perfectly well on our own.

What do YOU think?

Glossary

acquaintance someone you meet in your daily life but who you don't know very well

bully to pick on someone and treat them cruelly and unfairly

cancer serious disease in which some cells in the body produce harmful growths

carer someone who looks after children, but is not their parent

communicate talking to someone and listening carefully to what they have to say

cooperative being helpful and respectful towards other people

extended family wider family, which may include grandparents, aunts, uncles and cousins, as well as parents, brothers, sisters and step-families

personal certain things about someone's life or their family and friends that are private to them

personality the kind of person you are and the way you behave

respect treat someone as if their feelings and opinions are important

self-esteem to like and value yourself

sibling brother or sister

step-brother son of a step-parent

step-family a parent's new wife, husband or partner, and his or her children and relatives

step-sister daughter of a step-parent

step-parent new wife, husband or partner of a child's parent

threaten when someone scares someone else by saying that they will do something nasty to them in the future

value to like someone or something and appreciate their good points

Check it out

Check out these books and websites to find out more about relationships, and to get help and advice.

Books
Non-fiction
Get Real: Coping with Families, Kate Tym (Raintree, 2004)

Get Real: Coping with Friends and Relations, Kate Tym (Raintree, 2004)

The Girls' Book of Friendship: Cool Quotes, True Stories, Secrets and More, Catherine Dee (Little Brown and Co, 2001)

Fiction
Buried Alive, Jacqueline Wilson (Doubleday, 1999)

Best Friends, Jacqueline Wilson (Doubleday, 2004)

Websites
Children's Express: http://www.childrens-express.org/dynamic/public/library_family_relationships.htm

BBCNewsround: http://news.bbc.co.uk/cbbcnews/hi/chat/your_comments/newsid_3247000/3247148.stm

ChildLine: http://www.childline.org.uk (then type the word 'friends' to search the website)

Getting help
If you are worried about your relationships with friends or family, you may want to phone a helpline for support.

- In the UK, you can call ChildLine on 0800 11 11 (open 24 hours a day). Please remember that calls to 0800 numbers are free, and they do not show up on phone bills. You can also write to them at ChildLine, Freepost NATN 1111, London, E1 6BR

- In Australia, you can phone Kids Help Line on 1800 551800 (open 24 hours a day)

Titles in the *Get Wise* series include:

Hardback   0 431 21032 2

Hardback   0 431 21003 9

Hardback   0 431 21004 7

Hardback   0 431 21002 0

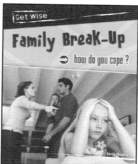

Hardback   0 431 21035 7

Hardback   0 431 21033 0

Hardback   0 431 21036 5

Hardback   0 431 21000 4

Hardback   0 431 21001 2

Hardback   0 431 21034 9

Find out about other titles from Heinemann Library on our website
www.heinemann.co.uk/library